Date: 3/3/16

J 635 RIS
Rissman, Rebecca,
Urban farming /

URBAN FARMING

by Rebecca Rissman

Content Consultant
Susan Oh, MS, MPH, RD, LD
Director, Research Nutrition Program
John Hopkins School of Medicine

Core Library

An Imprint of Abdo Publishing
abdopublishing.com

abdopublishing.com

Published by Abdo Publishing, a division of ABDO, PO Box 398166,
Minneapolis, Minnesota 55439. Copyright © 2016 by Abdo Consulting
Group, Inc. International copyrights reserved in all countries. No part of
this book may be reproduced in any form without written permission from
the publisher. Core Library™ is a trademark and logo of Abdo Publishing.

Printed in the United States of America, North Mankato, Minnesota
042015
092015

THIS BOOK CONTAINS
RECYCLED MATERIALS

Cover Photo: Benjamin Beytekin/Picture-Alliance/DPA/AP Images
Interior Photos: Benjamin Beytekin/Picture-Alliance/DPA/AP Images,
1; Jared Ramsdell/Journal Inquirer/AP Images, 4; Red Line Editorial, 8;
Richard B. Levine/Newscom, 10, 18; Horace Cort/AP Images, 14; Carlos
Osorio/AP Images, 16, 24; Phil Clarke Hill/In Pictures/Corbis, 21; John
Braid/Shutterstock Images, 23, 45; Richard Vogel/AP Images, 26; Peter
Bennett/Danita Delimont Photography/Newscom, 29; Mark Weber/The
Commercial Appeal/AP Images, 31; iStockphoto, 33, 39, 41; Shutterstock
Images, 36

Editor: Mirella Miller
Series Designer: Becky Daum

Library of Congress Control Number: 2015931589

Cataloging-in-Publication Data
Rissman, Rebecca.
 Urban farming / Rebecca Rissman.
   p. cm. -- (Food matters)
Includes bibliographical references and index.
ISBN 978-1-62403-868-6
1. Urban agriculture--Juvenile literature.   I. Title.
635.9--dc23
                                                    2015931589

CONTENTS

CHAPTER ONE
City Farms   4

CHAPTER TWO
The History of
Urban Farming   10

CHAPTER THREE
How Urban Farms Function   18

CHAPTER FOUR
The Perks and Pitfalls of
Urban Farming   26

CHAPTER FIVE
Urban Farming and Your Life   36

Just the Facts 42

In the Kitchen 43

Stop and Think 44

Glossary 46

Learn More 47

Index 48

About the Author 48

CITY FARMS

A farmer wakes up bright and early to work the land. She pulls weeds, trims plants, and carefully waters her soil. She picks some of the ripest tomatoes and cucumbers to sell at the market later in the day. In these ways, she is a typical farmer. However she is also unique. Instead of driving to her farm, she takes the subway. Her farm is not

A growing number of farms and gardens around the world are starting in urban areas.

located in the countryside. It is in the middle of a bustling city. She is an urban farmer.

What Is Urban Farming?

Urban farming is the practice of raising food inside a city's limits. It is not a new idea. Urban farming has been around for thousands of years. Archaeologists discovered evidence that ancient Maya people practiced urban farming more than 2,000 years ago. They farmed crops inside their cities. Ancient Romans who had small herb gardens in their villas were urban farmers too. In the past few decades, however, urban farming has become increasingly popular. Many people see it as a way to grow fresh, healthy food.

Urban farms can range in size from very small to quite large. Some provide only enough food to supplement a family's groceries. A family might keep a container garden on their apartment balcony. This is a very small-scale type of urban farming. Other urban farms are so big they produce enough food to be sold at local markets.

Food Deserts

In some urban areas, it is difficult to buy fresh produce. There may be only a few grocery stores, or the stores that exist may sell only very small amounts of fruits and vegetables. These urban areas are called "food deserts." Cities such as New Orleans, Louisiana, and Chicago, Illinois, have some of the worst food deserts in the United States. People who live in food deserts often suffer health problems, such as obesity or diabetes. Some cities are tackling the problem of food deserts with urban farms. Schools, churches, and

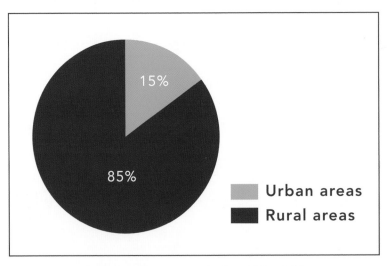

Where Is Food Raised around the World?
This pie chart shows where most of the world's food is raised. Some countries grow nearly all of their food in cities. Other countries, such as the United States, grow most of their food in rural areas. Ask an adult to help you research online some of the urban farming techniques used in places such as Singapore, London, and Paris.

volunteer organizations work together to grow fresh food in urban environments. They sell the fruits and vegetables locally. Nearby residents can purchase and eat these fresh, healthy food choices.

While most farms are found in rural areas, urban farming is becoming more popular each year. Urban farmers can enjoy the process of growing their own food and the good health that comes from eating it.

In war-torn Syria, urban farms are helping residents feed one another. In this excerpt from an article in *Al-Monitor*, a young man named Suleiman talks about how he turned to urban farming to provide food for his hometown if it was ever attacked:

> My friend and I were wondering what we could possibly do if Aleppo was besieged. We got the idea of building large farms that cater to the people's animal-product needs. But, nobody adopted the project, so we reduced its scale, and I found that my deserted house would be the perfect place for it. . . . I plant vegetables so that we can have food to face hunger. My family is poor, and my father is crippled, as he was wounded in the shelling . . . This garden will get us through the tough times, but I do not know if it will be enough in case we find ourselves under siege.

> Source: Mohammed Al-Khatieb. "Besieged Aleppo Residents Turn to Farming." Al-Monitor. Al-Monitor, December 11, 2014. Web. Accessed February 4, 2015.

Point of View

After reading this excerpt, consider how Suleiman's point of view is different from that of this book's author. How does Suleiman describe the purpose of his urban farm? Is it different or similar to the way the author describes urban farms in Chapter One? How does Suleiman's perspective change the way you think about urban farms?

CHAPTER TWO

THE HISTORY OF URBAN FARMING

People have been planting and caring for urban farms for thousands of years. In addition to the ancient Maya civilization and Rome, urban farming flourished in France. From the 1500s through the 1900s, urban farmers in Paris practiced the French-intensive style of growing food. This method was extremely successful. Parisian farmers grew vegetables in small, raised garden boxes. The city was

People in charge of urban gardens rely on manure and compost piles to fertilize their crops.

Start Composting

Many urban farms use compost to fertilize their soil. Compost is broken down natural matter. Set a 4- to 5- gallon (15 to 19 L) bucket near your back door. Place a smaller bucket filled with soil next to it. Collect your uneaten food scraps each day, and dump them in the large bucket. You can compost fruits, vegetables, old bread, grains, and eggshells. Make sure you do not compost meat, bones, dairy products, or grease. Sprinkle soil on top of the food scraps. This helps the compost decay. Keep a lid on the bucket. Soon the food scraps will decay and become a moist, brown mixture. You can use this mixture to fertilize your urban garden.

jam-packed with horses for riding and pulling carts. So the farmers used horse manure to fertilize their soil. Many modern farmers across the world still use manure today.

Organic farmers do not use chemical fertilizers. Instead they use natural fertilizers, such as manure. Unlike chemical fertilizers, which are made from manufactured elements, natural fertilizers come from organic sources, such as rotting plant matter and animal droppings. Compost is a natural material that organic and urban farmers often use to keep their soil healthy. It is made from decaying waste materials, such as vegetable scraps and paper.

More recently, urban farming has played an important role in many different parts of the world, including the United States. In the 1800s, breweries in New York raised livestock to help deal with their trash. They kept cows in pens near their breweries. They fed the cows the leftover grains used to brew beer. The cows then provided much of New York's milk supply.

Patriotic Gardens

World War I (1914–1918) and World War II (1939–1945) stretched US food production sources thin. US leaders urged citizens to become involved with urban farming to help with the lack of food sources. During World War I, President Woodrow Wilson encouraged Americans to grow liberty gardens. These were small gardens where homemakers could grow their own food to eat. During World War II, Americans were encouraged

For many children during World War I and World War II, after-school chores included working in the family's victory garden.

to grow victory gardens. These were similar to liberty gardens, and they helped reduce food costs. Even the White House had a victory garden.

Urban Farming Is Reborn

In the years after the wars, urban farming became less popular. Advances in transportation meant food could be moved quickly by train, ship, or truck. Refrigeration technology also advanced. Many families were able to purchase freezers for their homes. Farmers could now freeze their produce. This meant food could be grown, frozen, and then shipped from great distances.

In the 1970s, urban farming experienced a rebirth. Economic troubles in big cities, such as Detroit, Michigan, and Milwaukee, Wisconsin, led some companies and families to move away. This left abandoned plots of land inside the cities. Urban farmers began to

Depression Relief Gardens

In the 1930s, the United States experienced an economic collapse known as the Great Depression. At the most desperate time, between 13 and 15 million Americans were unemployed. People struggled to buy food. During this time, urban farming became a necessary part of survival. In many areas, people grew nutritious vegetables in subsistence gardens. These gardens were not meant to be profitable or to feed a large group of people. They were intended to help a family survive hard times. In many big cities, work-relief gardens paid small wages for people to work. These gardens solved two problems: they helped people find employment and also provided much-needed food.

Residents in present-day Detroit have transformed some of the city's many empty lots into community gardens.

use these plots for growing food. As a result, urban farms became an important part of life in cities stretching from New York City to Oakland, California.

In this excerpt, Elizabeth Hughes Smith, a resident of Biloxi, Mississippi, during World War II tells of her struggles and successes growing a victory garden:

> We started out with some tomato plants, but the worms got 'em all the time, so we kind of gave up on those, and then my mother, was the gardener, and she planted some snap beans and we had success with those. And some yellow squash, and they grew very nicely in the backyard. . . .
>
> The victory garden was fun. It did give us some fresh vegetables. And my mother had a farmer who laughed at us . . . he would come and bring vegetables and fresh honey and hand churned butter to us. But he would laugh at our struggles with our victory garden. But we were determined. We were a very patriotic family. And we were determined to grow something that we could eat and say we had a victory garden.

Source: Elizabeth Hughes Smith. "Oral Histories." The Classroom Victory Garden Project. *The National WWII Museum*, n.d. Web. Accessed February 4, 2015.

What's the Big Idea?

Read this passage closely. What is Smith's main point? Choose one or two details that support her main point. Which details stand out about her memory of growing a victory garden?

HOW URBAN FARMS FUNCTION

I n many cities, rooftop gardens, balcony planters, and backyard chicken coops are regular sights. Urban farming is a common way for city dwellers to grow food to eat or sell. But how does urban farming work?

Urban farms have a few simple needs: access to sunlight, space, soil, and water. City farmers often find these things in unexpected places. To find space and

Rooftops are a convenient location for small-scale urban farms.

Vertical Farming

Vertical farming is a new type of urban farming technology. Traditional farming methods use large plots of flat land. Vertical farming uses small areas of flat land inside tall buildings. In Sweden there is a 12-story greenhouse called the Plantagon. Trays of vegetable plants are moved through the greenhouse from the top floor to the bottom. By the time the plants reach the basement level, they are ready to be harvested. In Chicago, a repurposed meatpacking facility called The Plant grows plants that float in rafts on water. Special lamps provide light to help the plants grow inside the three-story building.

sunlight, small-scale urban farms use empty side yards or shared rooftop spaces. Balconies, unused fire escapes, and window boxes are other places where city dwellers can grow food. Large-scale urban farms often use empty lots. In these areas, farmers grow fruits and vegetables. They also raise animals, such as goats, chickens, and bees.

Much of the soil found in cities is not suitable for growing plants. It lacks nutrients or contains pollutants. Harmful metals, such as

Vertical gardens are becoming increasingly popular in urban cities such as London.

YOUR LIFE

Visit an Urban Farm

Ask an adult to help you research a local urban farm online. Find out if it is open to the public. Then take a trip to the farm. When you get there, ask the farmer questions about the types of food grown on the farm, where the farm's water comes from, if the farmer uses compost, and where the farmer sells the farm's goods. Write down the farmer's answers.

lead or arsenic, often are found in urban soil. They can hurt humans or other animals that eat them. One way urban farmers solve this problem is by building raised garden beds. They buy soil from gardening stores or bring it in from rural areas. Farmers then keep their soil healthy with fertilizer and compost.

Many urban farmers buy fertilizers from gardening stores or use manure purchased from farms. Some farmers make their own compost. Others receive donated compost from restaurants or schools. These resources allow urban farmers to create their own safe, healthy soil for growing food.

Urban farmers fill raised garden beds with new, safe soil.

For small urban gardens, found on rooftops and balconies, people usually use their own tap water to keep their plants watered. This is not as simple for larger urban farms. Few large-scale urban farms have access to their own water sources. Farmers must work creatively to keep their plants watered. Some farmers use rainwater. They collect rainwater from rooftops using gutters that run into storage containers. Other

Urban farms require a lot of hard work from volunteers.

urban farms use water from nearby buildings that either donate it or charge the farmers a small fee.

Human Power

Unlike rural farms, urban farms are not run with heavy machinery. They are too small to need tractors and combines. Instead they are run with human power. Volunteers and farmers use hand tools to plant and harvest their crops. This work is often physically challenging. It is also time consuming.

Urban farms take a great deal of work. They must be maintained carefully. Farmers often are required to be creative when working in small spaces with few resources. However, they are also rewarded for their work. The food grown on urban farms is usually delicious, fresh, and healthy.

EXPLORE ONLINE

Chapter Three focuses on the science behind urban farming. It briefly touches on vertical farming. Check out the website at the link below. As you know, each source is different. How is the information in this chapter different from what you read on the website? How do the two sources present information differently?

Vertical Farming
mycorelibrary.com/urban-farming

THE PERKS AND PITFALLS OF URBAN FARMING

There are many benefits to urban farming. However, people often raise valid concerns about it too. Learning more about the good and bad parts of urban farming involves looking at economic, environmental, and social issues.

The financial benefits of urban farming are easy to see. Food prices are rising at grocery stores. Urban farming provides city dwellers with low-cost

Successful large-scale urban farms are able to sell their goods directly to consumers in their communities.

food. People who grow their own food often can do so without paying much money to get started. And urban farms often sell food at low prices to compete with local grocery stores. Buying food locally is good for city economies. Urban farmers sell their goods at farmers' markets or directly to consumers from their farms. This means shoppers buying from urban farms are contributing money back to their communities.

Environmentally Friendly Farming

Urban farms are good for the environment. They often reuse resources. Many use donated food

Creative Garden Spaces

Many urban farmers make use of unusual spaces to raise plants and animals. Some of them might surprise you. Small urban gardens are often found on unused fire escapes and inside traffic circles. They may also be found on balconies and in parking garages. Some farmers have even grown crops in the beds of their pickup trucks! In 2014 the San Francisco Giants opened an edible farm inside AT&T Park. The garden helps supply the park with healthy concession-stand food.

Urban gardens with rain barrels do not rely on city water sources.

scraps for their compost. They get these scraps from restaurants or grocery stores. This reduces the volume of food waste in local trash, which results in less trash being deposited in landfills. Some urban farms use collected rainwater to water their plants.

Another benefit of urban farming is that it minimizes the need to ship food from rural farms to cities. Urban farms grow food locally, which reduces transportation pollution from trucks, trains, and ships. It also uses less fuel. This is good for the environment, as fuel is a limited natural resource.

Volunteer Forces

Volunteer organizations operate many urban farms. These community groups educate their workers about how food is grown, cared for, and harvested. Many children living in urban environments have few chances to learn this information. Volunteering with a community group is a way for people to gain valuable skills. Urban farm volunteers learn to work with a team and communicate with customers, neighbors, and other volunteers. They also learn the basic skills needed to grow, nourish, and harvest edible plants.

Students who volunteer with urban farms can learn skills to be used later in life.

Issues with Urban Farms

One concern about urban farms is related to the safety of the food they produce. Urban farms come into contact with pollution. This pollution comes from cars, construction, and nearby factories. Food grown in polluted soil and water can make people sick. Garden beds are one solution for small-scale urban farms.

Large-scale urban farms must find other solutions to avoid polluted soil and water. Some farmers build a barrier between their crops and the soil. They lay concrete over the existing soil. Then they grow plants in fresh soil on top of the concrete. Another way to avoid pollution is to clean the soil. Farmers do this by growing plants, such as sunflowers, that absorb pollutants. Once the plants have grown, the farmers throw them away. When the soil has been cleaned, farmers grow food crops in the soil. Removing pollutants makes urban farms safer. But it can be time consuming and expensive.

Like soil, farmers must also test water to be sure it is not polluted. Urban water often contains pollutants, such as gasoline, lead, and chemicals from factories. Many urban farmers must buy fresh water that can be used to water their crops and feed their animals safely.

Another problem with urban farming is vandalism. Many urban farms are located in

Pollution and Urban Farms
This image shows how pollution can contaminate urban farms. As you can see, pollution from a construction site is very close to this farm. If this were your farm, how would you ensure your soil and water were clean and safe? Look back through this chapter for some ideas. Then write a plan for your clean urban farm.

high-crime neighborhoods. Vandals damage property or steal food and equipment when urban farms are unguarded. Rural farms also deal with incidents of vandalism but much less frequently. They are located in less-populated areas and on larger plots of land. This means vandals must work harder to inflict damage on rural farms.

Can Urban Farms Compare?

Urban farms are almost always much smaller than commercial farms. Commercial farms are large-scale operations. They often take up thousands of acres of rural land. Small, human-powered farms simply cannot compete with the output of rural, commercial farms. Urban farms are less efficient and grow less food.

Food production is an enormous industry. And it is very important too. The way food is grown and produced can impact the environment, as well as the health of the people who eat it. Urban farms produce a relatively small amount of the food consumed in the United States. The North American Urban Agriculture Committee estimates it is around 5 percent. Understanding the benefits and concerns of urban farms helps people decide if they would like to use goods that come from these small food sources. It also helps people decide if they would like to try farming too.

FURTHER EVIDENCE

Chapter Four discusses the pros and cons of urban farming. What are some of the chapter's main points? Which pieces of evidence support these points? Go to the website below. Does the information there support what you read in this chapter? Write a few sentences using new information from the website to support what you read in this chapter.

Growing a Green Future

mycorelibrary.com/urban-farming

CHAPTER FIVE

URBAN FARMING AND YOUR LIFE

Very few people around the world live on farms. Just 2 percent of Americans do. But this does not mean the remaining 98 percent of Americans cannot grow their own food. Urban farming is one way almost everyone can become involved in food production.

Growing your own food is an educational activity. Do not worry about finding an abandoned city lot.

It is easy and inexpensive to start a small indoor garden.

Many fruits and vegetables are shipped long distances. Often they are picked before they are ripe. They then ripen as they arrive at their destination. Some vegetables and fruits picked before they ripen are less nutritious than those allowed to fully ripen on the plant. Red peppers that reach ripeness while on the plant have higher levels of vitamin C than those picked early. Produce also often loses nutrients while being transported. To get the most nutrients from food, buy fruits and vegetables from your local farmers' market or urban farm that are picked only when fully ripe. Then eat them right away.

Instead start small. Look around your home for a safe, sunny spot. It might be on a windowsill or on your back porch.

Once you have found your location, decide what you want to grow. Good options are small potted plants, such as herbs or peppers. Ask an adult to help you buy seeds and soil from a local gardening store or supermarket. Then either plant your garden directly in the ground or use a recycled food container as a planter. Follow the growing directions on

It is important to eat a wide variety of fruits and vegetables to keep a healthy diet.

your seed packets. Soon you will have a small garden growing.

Not everyone has access to seeds and potting soil. If you cannot grow your own food, don't worry. You can still do your part to help urban farms. Ask your parents if you can visit a local urban farm or farmers' market. Giving urban farms your business is one way you can help support them.

Do the Math

Growing your own food can help you save money. Make a list of the items you would need to set up a small urban garden. Then write down the price of each item. Your list might look like this:

Packet of tomato seeds: $3.25

Potting soil: $4.50

Recycled container: $0

Total price: $7.75

Then ask your parents to estimate how much money they spend each month on tomatoes. Their estimate might look like this:

Tomato cost per month: 2 pounds (0.9 kg) at $2.50 per pound = $5 a month

$5 x 12 months = $60

Yearly savings:

$60 - $7.75 = $52.25

Get Healthy

Growing your own food and supporting local farms can help you eat healthier foods. Eating fresh fruits and vegetables is an important part of a healthy, balanced diet. Children between the ages of 9 and 13 should eat 2 to 2.5 cups of vegetables each day.

When most people picture farms, they think of rolling hills and open, country spaces. However farms and gardens also can be found between buildings, on apartment balconies, and on

Growing your own food or buying from another urban garden is a great way to bring healthy foods into your diet.

rooftops. These urban farms and gardens often are quite small. Yet their impact is big. They educate people about how to grow vegetables. They help the environment. And they provide city dwellers with fresh, locally grown produce, meat, dairy, and honey.

- Urban farming involves farming inside a city. Urban farmers can raise fruits, vegetables, grains, and herbs. They also can raise livestock, such as chickens and goats. Some urban farmers can raise bees for honey.
- Urban farming is a very old tradition. Archaeologists have found evidence of Maya urban farms.
- Urban farmers have four needs: sunlight, space, soil, and water. Once they have these, they can raise plants and animals to eat or sell.
- Urban farming has many benefits. It is good for the environment. It gives consumers low-cost options for healthy, fresh food. It reuses resources, such as water and food scraps. And it provides opportunities for volunteering.
- There are many concerns about urban farms. Vandals often target them. Pollution in city soil and water can contaminate plants and animals, which can harm the humans who eat them. Urban farms are not as efficient or productive as commercial farms.

IN THE KITCHEN

Grow Your Own Herb Garden

- Potting soil
- 4 medium-sized plastic containers, such as yogurt tubs
- 1 marker
- 4 types of herb seeds, such as basil, dill, rosemary, and chive
- Water
- A sunny spot, such as a windowsill

Fill each container three-quarters full with potting soil. Read the directions on the seed packets and plant a different herb in each container. Mark each container with the name of the herb it contains. Place the containers in a sunny spot and water the seeds daily. Once the seeds have grown, use the herbs to season your food. Try the basil in scrambled eggs. Sprinkle rosemary on potatoes. Try dill on raw tomatoes. Add chopped chives to roasted chicken.

STOP AND THINK

You Are There

Chapter Two discusses the history of urban farming, including some of the early advances made in Paris. Imagine you are a child living in Paris in the 1500s. You need to grow food for your family. How will you do it? Will you move to the countryside, or will you grow an urban garden? What special steps will you take to make sure your vegetables grow well?

Another View

This book has information about how urban farms provide fresh, healthy food choices. However, as you know, every source is different. Ask an adult, such as a librarian, to help you find another source about urban farming. Research and then write a short essay comparing and contrasting the new source's point of view with that of this book's author. What is each author's point of view? How are their views similar or different, and why?

Why Do I Care?

Urban farms make up a small percentage of the total number of farms in the United States. Do they have any effect on your life? Are there any parts of urban farming that might impact you? How do you think urban farming changes the environment inside cities?

Take a Stand

This book talks about the positive and negative sides to urban farming. Imagine you are shopping for vegetables. Would you prefer to buy them from an urban farm or from a rural farm? Write a short essay explaining your decision. Make sure to give the reasons for your decision, as well as facts to back it up.

GLOSSARY

breweries
companies that produce beer

combines
large pieces of farm
machinery that help cut and
clean grain crops

commercial
related to a business

compost
broken-down matter used to
keep soil healthy

contaminate
exposing something to
harmful matter

fertilizer
a substance that is added to
soil and helps plants grow

homemakers
people who manage their
household as their principal
job

manure
animal droppings used for
fertilizer

pollution
something that has harmful
effects on the environment

produce
goods that have been grown,
such as fruits or vegetables

rural
related to the countryside

subsistence gardens
gardens that provide almost
all the food required by a
family

LEARN MORE

Books

Fox, Thomas. *Urban Farming.* Irvine, CA: BowTie Press, 2011.

Smith, Jeremy N. *Growing a Garden City.* New York: Skyhorse Publishing, 2010.

Wood, Kelly. *Urban Farm Projects: Making the Most of Your Money, Space, and Stuff.* Irvine, CA: I-5 Publishing, 2014.

Websites

To learn more about Food Matters, visit **booklinks.abdopublishing.com**. These links are routinely monitored and updated to provide the most current information available.

Visit **mycorelibrary.com** for free additional tools for teachers and students.

INDEX

abandoned lots, 15–16, 20, 37

balcony gardens, 7, 19–20, 23, 28, 40

chemical fertilizers, 12, 22
chicken coops, 6, 19
compost, 12–13, 22, 29

food deserts, 7
food miles, 34
food prices, 27–28, 40
food waste, 29
freezers, 15

garden beds, 11, 22, 31

herb gardens, 6

large-scale farms, 7, 20, 23, 32, 34
liberty gardens, 13–14

manure, 12, 22
Maya civilization, 6, 11

Paris, France, 8, 11–12
Plant, The, 20
Plantagon, 20
pollutants, 20, 32
pollution, 30, 31–32, 33, 34

rainwater, 23, 29
refrigeration, 14–15
Romans, 6, 11
rooftop gardens, 19–20, 23, 41

small-scale farms, 7, 13–14, 20, 23, 28, 31, 34, 40
soil, 5, 12–13, 19–20, 22, 31–32, 33, 38–39, 40
subsistence gardens, 15

transportation, 14, 30, 34, 38

vandalism, 32–33
vertical farming, 20, 25
victory gardens, 14, 17
volunteers, 8, 24–25, 30

water, 6, 19, 20, 22, 23–24, 29, 31–32, 33

ABOUT THE AUTHOR

Rebecca Rissman is an award-winning children's author and editor. She has written more than 200 books about history, culture, science, and art. She lives in Portland, Oregon, with her husband and daughter.